FORTY DAYS

Poetry by
David Kaiser

Artwork by
Richard Nostbakken

EPIPHANY
B O O K S

Published by Aurora Productions
Regina, Saskatchewan, Canada

FORTY DAYS

Copyright © 1993 by David Kaiser.

The poem "Bit Parts" (page 49) is reprinted by permission from REJOICE, Grade 9, Quarter 3, © 1992 Augsburg Fortress.

Scripture quotations are from the *Revised Standard Version of the Bible*, copyright 1946, 1952, and 1971, by the Division of Christian Education of the National Council of Churches of Christ in the United States of America.

Publishing Editor: Dennis D. Hendricksen
Watercolour Painting and Line Drawings by Richard Nostbakken.
Graphic Design, Typesetting and Page Icons by George E. Flengeris.
Body of text typeset in Times New Roman.
This book was created electronically using Aldus PageMaker® 4.0.
Icons and special typographic effects rendered with CorelDRAW® 3.0.
Printed and bound in Canada by Printco Graphics - Regina, Sask.

ISBN 0-9697164-0-0

Epiphany Books
Published by
Aurora Productions
P.O. Box 1072
Regina, Saskatchewan
Canada   S4P 3B2

Dedicated
to my family
who patiently listen
to my many
words.

CONTENTS

Preface   *vi*
Foreword   *vii*

CREATIONS

what if   2
noah   3
paper folder   4
Three wishes for circles   5
Creation Continued   6
The walls are thick   7
walls   8
Spirit Fruit   9

INCARNATIONS

In pursuit of Gabriel   11
seeds   12
Christmas Toys   13
journeys   14
no vacancy   15
fallen birds and dying worlds   16
untitled   17
Pieced Quilts   17
incarnation et al   18

CONFESSIONS

Imitation   20
cain   21
Complaint of Wilderness Wanderers   22
forward   23
whitewash   24
Prophets without honour   25
The Pharisee and the Boa   26
internal securities   27
1 Corinthians 11   28
struggles   29
doorway dancers   30

HOLY WEEKS AND OTHER TIMES

ash wednesday 1	32
ash wednesday 2	34
Rubrics	36
sunday first	38
monday tuesday wednesday	39
supper on thursday	40
friday	41
echo	42
saturday	43
sunday two	44

FOLLOWERS

a most recent matthew	46
the minstrel sang	47
wild roses	48
Bit Parts	49
euangelion (good news)	50
(euloge) - well-spoken	51
the little clown	52

CELEBRATIONS

celebrations	54
the juggler	55
potted plant	56
joy notes	57
dances of the children	58
Transfigurations	59

Scriptural Index	60
Liturgical Index	60
Topical Index	61
About the Poet	62
About the Artist	63

PREFACE

David Kaiser is in love with words and people. This new collection reflects both of these loves. His words shape his unerring belief that faith comes out of our lives, out of the mud of our sins. The images reflect his sense of possibilities in everyday things like bubbles and clowns and sad faces, and the possibility of words helping us see the hope and joy in ourselves. We are the "poor and hungry clowns and fools" (in "no vacancy") who need love and affirmation.

The poetry also helps us phrase the hard questions when faith doesn't always make sense. In "fallen birds and dying worlds" the speaker wonders, "how it came about/ that birds and boys and worlds all die". Here, too, is another element of his work: the juxtapositioning of the usual with the unusual to startle us. The mundane things of our lives stand beside the details of biblical lives giving us a chance to see ourselves differently. We take on the wandering of the Israelites whose "wandering is but new slavery/excluding the salad bar". ("Complaint of Wilderness Wanderers")

The delight in reading this poetry is that in showing us our sins, David also leads us to know that it is with joy that we find meaning in our lives. The jugglers, clowns, old men and children laugh in his poetry and we should laugh too. These poems urge us to do the joyful thing - be the joyful people of God. Read and be glad!

Angela Terpstra
Lecturer in English
Luther College, Regina, Sask.

FOREWORD

The number forty appears often in the Bible. Whether it be forty days and nights of rain, forty years of preparation for leadership, forty long years wandering in a wilderness, or forty days of contemplation and temptation, the writers of the biblical story note the days and years. Time is of the essence. It seems a certain amount of spent time is necessary in the plan of God to bring about completion, be it for individuals or nations.

This collection of poems will take some time to read, but more time to internalize. In a fast world, where we rush about, often without direction, it is not only helpful, but necessary to cultivate a contemplative spirit. It is hoped that the poems and related scripture passages will help the reader to that end. Take some time, forty days perhaps, and walk awhile among the words.

Readers, please note the indices at the back of the book. It provides a tool for using the poems at appropriate times during the year, as well as offers some suggestions of themes to which the poems may apply.

David Kaiser

"Creation - happens to us, burns into us, changes us, we tremble and swoon, we submit. Creation - we participate in it, we encounter it, we encounter the creator, offer ourselves to God, helpers and companions."

Martin Buber

CREATIONS

Jeremiah 33:6-11

what if

as vonnegut suggests
the film could be shown backwards
then the bullets would suck out
of the open wounds and jam back
in hot gun barrels and the guns
would melt down in furnaces
finally cooling in long trains
to be hauled back to the mines
where miners would hide them
under ground
in simple ore
and the acid in the dead lakes
would rise in reversed rain
forming clouds then smoke
pouring down the chimneys
materializing to coal and oil
to be unrefined and put back
in prehistoric swamps
to live
i could turn time around
to a warm womb further to egg
and sperm divided into generations
passing to the primordial adam
standing in eden
by choice or knowledge
where god could say
it is good

but then

there could be no love
for love is only possible
to the impossible
so let the film advance

CREATIONS

Genesis 8:18-22

noah

boat builder
teach us how the world ends
speak your past tense words
for present times
speak calming words
float them over waves
of tears and fears
to land us on a world
remade

the one we have
is again destroyed
by some who make the claim
that they are gods with right
and privilege
so to do

noah
favoured one
we have lost the instructions
for building arks
ships and canoes
so teach us how
and teach us who
so we might learn
to build again

CREATIONS

Psalm 139:1-18

paper folder

mostly i'm like poet's paper
   not so much white as experimental
   often discarded
   for the poems are seldom finish....
   the sentences end in mid....
piece after peace is thrown   away away   away

crumbled
  ripped
    discarded
      i rattle to the bottom
of any next to me waste place
sometimes i bounce off walls
then shred into tiny fr ag
  me   n   t   s
blown about by a wind of no hope

all of the above with appropriate
  exasperation
    expletives
      et ceteras

then he comes
  paints a design
   on my basic monochrome
     folds me on proper lines
     gives me wings
     and lets me fly

CREATIONS

Ephesians 4:1-16

Three wishes for circles

I wish for one small circle
   in the great design
   with softer edge
   than these precise squares I see.

I wish for released creativity
   from electronic exactness
   whose existence depends
   upon ninety degrees
   and four squared measured sides.

I wish my world discovered round
   not cubic
   nor in boxes
   of neat design
   and denominational orthodoxy.

CREATIONS

Genesis 1:31-2:3
Revelation 21:1-5a

Creation Continued

The original designs,
though bearing the God stamp of approval
were not accepted.
Six days creation redone in one,
bringing back the chaos
void and black-
an ultimate "no" to original questions.

Then God weeps.
And would it take a million years
to wash it clean with love filled tears,
God could and would begin again,
again, again and yet again.

Isaiah 35

The walls are thick in this room where I live.

Like midnight bats, my thoughts flit fast crashing on the
walls.
Black threats tangle my dreams.
Scenes flick by like B grade movies. My head hurts.
I cannot focus.
Errors haunt me. One hundred indiscretions laugh loud
on my face like playground bullies.
Failings that bite at my heels are untamed dogs of truth.
Broken promises hang like torn curtains in vacant
rooms.
Long awaited love words crumble and blow too late too late
piling against the winter.
It makes less sense than paper airplanes.
All around the innocent die with carefully designed reasons.
The room is empty like my broken heart.

Now I lay me down to sleep.....But my eyes stay open staring
at the walls papered with many myths. The walls are thick in
this room where I live.

I wish for the coyote to lick my hand.
I dream of a lion asleep by my bed.
I listen for birdsong in the morning.

Then somehow from somewhere like a dim memory another sound--
beyond the walls and the eyes. It beats.
There an irregular pounding pound pounding rhythms loud
of some forgotten unity, when all was one and right.

Suddenly there is a strange sound,...sight....who knows?

It struggles through the deep
from some womb-memory.

It sparkles. It sings. It shines.
The myths on the walls change from dull black and white
to colour, from flat and formal to all dimensional.
Then one word is shouted, Yes!

CREATIONS

Galatians 5:1

walls

i want stone walls not brick
walls where corners are not necessary
where small pieces are picked to fit
where square pegs in round holes
are not psychologically or otherwise
out of place and sync
a poem that doesn't rhyme

give me walls that take time to build
where masons search through rubble
roll and tumble stones ready to toss
some like salt over their shoulders
with whispered wish words
and wonder dreams
rumbling free in their minds

i don't want bricks on bricks
squared in orthodox codes
every one precise and proper
aligned and level (headed)
so they look straight and true
plus perfect from the street
giving everyone stiff necks

i will build my house
of field stones two feet thick
paint it puce add one red brick
so passers by will see the difference
then i will leave some secret nooks
where field mice can nest
and have their babies

Colossians 3:12-17

Spirit Fruit

Crutches for poets
this spirit fruit,
served at banquets for kings
and shared by paupers and beggars.

Fruit of sweetness
fruit of taste are
God symbols for life,
parameters for dying.

Fruit for itinerants
who come to pick something
better and fresh
from trees of life.

INCARNATIONS

"...And all this that our hunger might be fed, our dryness moistened, our weakness comforted, our iniquity quenched, our charity kindled."

St. Augustine of Hippo

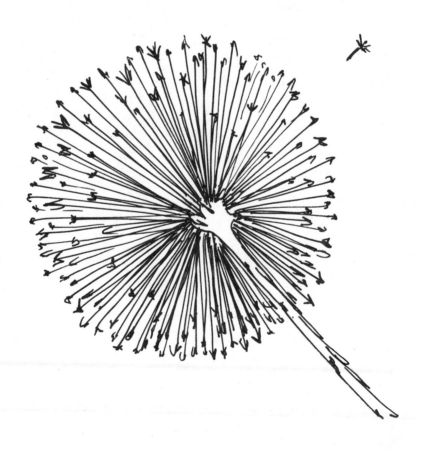

Matthew 1:18-25
Luke 1:26-45

In pursuit of Gabriel

Oh, if he would appear again
Heavenly messenger bringing news
Of births and gifts
Announcing virgins.
If I could but catch me one
with wings and songs,
then change the lyrics.

How does one catch an angel?
Do they only come to unsuspecting
virgins in their sleep wondering
if it was all a nightmare?
Does one need first to be engaged
to keeping laws perfectly?
Or do angels do their best breaking
through our dreams
announcing births that make no sense
setting all the world on edge?

11

INCARNATIONS

Luke 1:23-38

seeds

mary and elizabeth
enlarged with religion
by age and biology
impossible
met
the babies leapt
dandelions grew

grim herods wrote laws
seeking eradication

John 1:1-14

Christmas Toys

In the Land of silver cycles
    On oaken shelves with walnut beams
Stand rows and rows of wind-up toys
    Created from a master's dreams.

Deep in each wood and metal toy
    The master placed a clock-work spring
That wound up tight by a Child's hands
    Would cause the toy to dance and sing.

Although the toys were made to move,
    Like sculptured statues gathering dust
They stand unused. Ignored.
    Forgotten unto dust and rust.

The land had aged, grown grey and old.
    Its children would not play again.
Born as babes, but never young -
    Born to dust and acid rain.

No one knew the toys were there.
    Their purpose lost. They brought no joy.
They waited in cobwebbed silence, waited
    The wonder touch of a girl or boy.

With saddened heart, the master saw
    The toys he'd made. Unused until
Someone there would care and play.
    Knowing none, he said, "I will."

And so a child was born who laughed
    Through wanton waste, through war and wrong.
He wound one toy, then two, then all.
    The toys and child began a song.

Throughout the land few understood
    Why forgotten toys began to move.
Their tick-tock hearts beat loud with life
    Recreated by his touch of love.

INCARNATIONS

Jeremiah 35:15-17

*"So Joseph got up, took the child
and his mother during the night
and left for Egypt."* Matthew 1:14

journeys

firemen come
demanding unreal trees
crashing through our christmas
with threats of no insurance
for more than two or under
ecologist cry
murder on murderers
of trees the spruce balsam pine
and fir while cutting seventeen
to publish pleas for plastic solutions
economists rest
easy in the hope of thirty days
seeking heaven in november or december
but all betrayed in silver coins
people buy
their forest smells in aerosol can
with odours fooling minds and noses
then spray sweet wishes deep in corners
of each living room
it culminates
in quick march flight
while searching stable silence
where white doves whisper soft
and children safely sleep
they dream
green trees with imaginative alternatives
where emperors and kings decree peace
and little
ones no
longer
hide

14

INCARNATIONS

Isaiah 42:18-22, 43:1-13

no vacancy

our five star inns are rated now
by baths and bars and pillowed rooms
with cabled fun and compact discs
tuned loud against the nighttime gloom

no vacancy is neon flashed
so tired travellers drive on by
and we avoid their weary eyes
ignore their deepest questioned why

first come first served if right reserved
no room to spare for midnight guests
we police with night locks bravely set
and guarantee a good night's rest

restrictive building codes apply
with warning signs no kids allowed
nor starving tired mothers here
we've room for only happy crowds

then late one night one risks all
comes to birth in the parking shed
beside a smelly refuse bin
with no soft pillow for his head

we meet him in the morning cold
he speaks of change and peace to all
and light for warmth in the winter grey
like one did once in a stable stall

he seeks to find a welcome here
to break our harsh forbidding rules
to open hearts with giving love
for poor and hungry clowns and fools

INCARNATIONS

Isaiah 61:1-9

fallen birds and dying worlds

she held the tiny dust brown bird
in her gentle mother hand
it's dead she said through tender tears
her whys and mine could not understand
why birds or puppies have to die

the mother held the dust brown boy
his swollen belly a mystery
cold irony of the underfed
we starve and still i cannot see
why sons or mothers have to die

god held the broken dust brown earth
heard the noise of profane shout
smelled the breath of putrid fumes
and wondered how it came about
that birds and boys and worlds all die

so he came to dust brown town
sharing blood and bread with pain
admitting whys but bringing hope
that nothing ever will be the same
when birds and boys and worlds die

Mark 10:13-16

untitled

The danger is that when we are out
of the room he will be born again
in the present tense
And there will be no instant replays
for possible analysis at reverse angles
with slow motion projection and chalk
pointing out what we missed
All conveniently available to assist
us absent ones understand or at least
catch up with all the news
and whatever wednesdays and other days
happened
For in this christmas case
there are no new video releases for rent
after december 15 for one day only
nor will there ever be
since the story is always
incomprehensibly
now

Pieced Quilts

In these tangled times
    the weaver lays thread
    on fragile thread
    of hope and love creating pieces

To quilt in rich patterns
    soft blankets
    to wrap around our stiff and tired
    shoulders
    and our sagging hearts.

INCARNATIONS

John 1:14

incarnation et al

no more central to life
    than the tomb
    so god came

no more necessary for grey
    than colour
    so dandelions grew

no more real to breath
    than death
    so god died

no more hope for winter
    than spring
    so dandelions bloom

"On a really clean tablecloth, the smallest speck of dirt annoys the eyes.
At high altitudes, a moment's self-indulgence may mean death."

Dag Hammarskjold

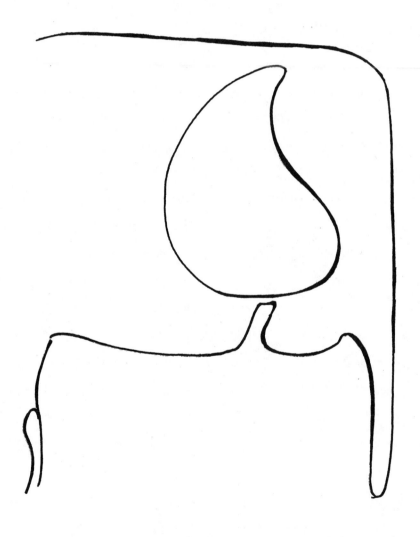

CONFESSIONS

Psalm 33:6-22

Imitation

I am Peter boasting even cross and life
damned by my denials.

I am Elisha begging every Elijah stay
the mantle off my back.

I am Moses shouting release and recall
with broken tongue and general ineptitude.

I am Cain making dead sure my brother
won't have other gifts.

I am Adam hiding in the garden bushes
passing blame eve on god.

I am chaos void of words
waiting yes from nothing.

CONFESSIONS

Psalm 37:7-11

cain

fugitive cain now you wander
ever moving from the question
never answered just denied

yet the blood spilled red is crying
loud and constant time repeated
in the night yes abel died

generations passed and passing
shouted questions over over
has our brother abel died

earth to earth they come the children
of the mothers asking asking
why oh why has abel died

generations pass on soft feet
marking distance from the crime
abel's dead yet still denied

CONFESSIONS

Exodus 16:1-12

Complaint of Wilderness Wanderers

It's not the manna.
It's the monotony
    and the Mondays.
Like sliced white bread three meals daily
    with double portions on Sundays.

O for the coriander, garlic and cucumbers,
The watermelon, leeks and fish,
    all we ever wanted.
We are used to such things now,
    where the children eat half price.

It's not the wilderness.
It's the memories reflected on the empty plates
    of former Egypts
That still rumble in our stomach pits,
    and tease the taste buds on our tongues.

We are sore distressed
In our feet, our minds, our appetites.
    We are used to more.
This wandering is but new slavery
    excluding the salad bar.

Numbers 14:1-9

forward

we cast such longing eyes
            in over-shoulder glances
      back
            to our former egypts
rebuking each inspired moses
who begs us leave
our water
and our graves

CONFESSIONS

Ezekiel 13:10-16

whitewash

i built my house of whitewash
against abuse advice and laughter
re-coated it annually brushing off
past days and dirt
it glistened white
and hurt the eyes
of those who happened by

when the storm blew in
hard on hard from the west
my house dissolved like dreams
then washed away
to deep and farther oceans

i stood stark naked
when the neighbours came
to view one more disaster
with usual questions and comments
about insurance
and enamel

Jeremiah 26
Luke 19:47-48

Prophets without honour

Seldom do we see them now, the prophets
Walking the streets of pain. They disappeared,
Some say, with the last bad news day
The anchored ones who hallow hurricanes and hate
On every noon and night and good good morning show,
Have our attention because they speak the truth
In eighteen seconds or less--
The whole truth--distilled and neat
Like whiskey--and nothing but the truth.
Spooned in easy to swallow capsules with promises of white
White teeth and sweet kiss breath.

Seldom do we see them now, the prophets,
Who they say hide in caves retreating
Into secrets better kept for times of understanding,
If they ever come again. There they spin their silence
Wool and flax to homespun cloth worn with wisdom.
But ignored, unhonoured by those who shop instead
For imported silk at bargain basement prices.

But they are there, the prophets,
Sometimes hiding in books and biographies
Myths and films crossing the mind with questions
And possibilities that maybe things do not have to stay
The same.

Yes, they are there, the prophets
Often recalling dead ancients whose hands
And feet knew soil, loved seeds and wrote songs
For several voices.

They are there, hanging old portraits
Along streets and sparing no expense
For children.

They are there, walking among the brand new action games.
If we only knew where to look.

25

CONFESSIONS

Matthew 23:1-28

The Pharisee and the Boa

When his eyes first spied the big boa coiled,
     His mouth went dry his throat constricted tight.
His feet said, "Run!" But his head said "Stop!"
     "You must remain religiously right."

So, with head in the clouds and stars in his eyes,
     He considered what was good for his soul.
While more earthly bound, the boa began nibbling his toes
     And swallowed him perfectly whole.

Luke 6:37-42

internal securities

we hide behind our triple locks
dead bolted against all entries
without invitation

we wire our windows
time our lights on or off
fooling neighbours cats and sparrows

but we are at home
ourselves ourselves
we eat with thieves and liars

wondering how they got in

C O N F E S S I O N S

1 Corinthians 11:27-29

Rightly discerning the rightly discerning
we sit making mental checks
marking each and every minor discrepancy
...unshined...shoes...unruly...hair
...children...music...sung off key
...silk slips showing...plain as sin.
Pious eyes squint n
           a
           r
           r
           o
           w in close
              certain
              scrutiny.

...so engrossed in selves...
...the banquet passes...
    unnoticed
    as the host.

Amos 6:1-6

struggles

they struggle inside me
the verbs begging action
a dichotomy of choices
to take my cross

to love my neighbours
i split four ways
between
me myself and i   plus   "you"

my living room widens
to a world of the tenth power
where young ones die
by diet drinks

i weep then for the children

CONFESSIONS

Romans 14:1-13

doorway dancers

they are dancing now in doorways
the narrow minded people
keeping music in and private

having long since learned
that doorways are safe

in earthquakes and tornados

"When you read what he said
It never stays on the pages,
...but the words glow and speak...
They step over aeons, march over ages,
They are not antlike marks on whispering pages!"

William Rose Benet

HOLY WEEKS AND OTHER TIMES

Psalm 13

ash wednesday 1

on ash wednesdays the catholic kids
came to school with smudged black crosses
right in the middle of their foreheads
they had been to early mass

we knew they had gone - for the school bus
was half empty and breakfast conversations
were full of our protestant parents
who were not sure we should see them

so we readied thick taunts and teases
to lay on the kids who went to church
went to church went to church
all on a wednesday morning

teachers glared us down and shook shame fingers
so we saved it all for recess
where the bravest ones laughed full hot
in the face of those they liked the least

the crosses stayed until noon
telling things that did with faith
and fathers mothers living still
who frightened us sometimes with sintalk

and godwrath because they said god knew
heard every word and saw us inside out
all around the mulberry bush the mulberry bush
so we could no longer hide

some of us went to church later that night
where hymns imposed instead of ashes
were sung in grey and heavy tones
since we had sore offended holy jesus

with nothing in our hands to bring
mere naked worms we creature things
to the lamb we came we came
for seven weeks without laughs or games

sometimes we wished for ashes
and crosses marking us upon our heads
better to see perhaps to believe
the words we heard of forgiveness

we envied st. joseph's church
with cloistered cells for confessings
where one could tell the truth
and not have the world blow up

Psalm 51

ash wednesday 2

it was most often in the solemn church
of black wool and sober farm faces
that the heaviness crushed me down
the weight of wearing david's name
was much too much to bear
and nothing seemed quite equal
(all have sinned and fallen...)
but lust is hardly born
in boys of six or seven
(though some would say it is)

it was most often under the stained
glass refracting light into rainbows
and pieces of verity and surety
that i knew god knew me
with the truth staring me down
like a playground bully
(in thought word and deed...)
even the uncommon hidden sins shouted
those known only by me and the other david
(with rubrics directing it all in red)

it was most often under the stern eyes
of the robed one who looked much like god
that i wished i was home
yet felt the basic honesty free me
in those repetitious spoken words
(to all who are truly repentant...)
which i was i was i was amen
thought no one else noticed but david and god
(the entire forgiveness of my sins...)

it was then the light shone through the windows
with a different inexplicable luminosity
that warmed me inside out
through the pure white shirt
all proper and starched for sundays
so i felt loved and held and kept
(and the ugly mural of jesus...)
painted on the north church wall
which had caused no small arguments
(changed...especially his eyes)

HOLY WEEKS AND OTHER TIMES

1 Peter 1:3-9

Rubrics

Earth may be cast on the coffin as the minister says,
"Ashes to ashes, dust to dust..."

Ashes are gathered
       by generals rewriting the story
       from front yard bright burning crosses,
       from deep dust hate lying mud thick,
       from children whose dreams die too young,
       from breasts that hang like dry winter fruit,
       from forests burned hot without rain,
       from hot furnaces spitting out steel;

Then imposed
       by a common perspective
       on the next to us near neighbour's house,
       on tall white fences writ in black signs,
       on detectors of motion at nighttime,
       on oak caskets paid for in quick plastic,
       on soil deprived of its growth soul
       of faces eroded with warm tears

"...in the sure and certain hope of..."

I like how they carefully end the late news.
       Yes, thank goodness for editors, humour and laughter.
           How else would we ever hope to cope?
       Too bad roses begin to wither on the way home.
Too bad no one goes to confession anymore.
           Everyone is waiting for someone to tell the truth.
It is quite the riddle this end of things, life, years, centuries.
How can ten year old murders be blamed
       on neighbourhoods and a mother's milk? I wonder.

CHORUS:
> *Ah, the grey ashes make for monotone Mondays,*
> *Thursdays come harder to breathe.*
> *The weeping does not wait for the morning.*
> *The kind words bring little relief.*

"...the resurrection of eternal life..."

New ashes cross peace on our foreheads
With words that ring old as forever.
Then from the ash heap a gold bird rises,
A tiny sunburst against the gathering why.
With wings reaching strong like the eagle,
It writes "yes" across the black sky.

HOLY WEEKS AND OTHER TIMES

Matthew 21:1-11

sunday first

with dreams of cowboy heroes
white stetsons dancing stallions
they crowd around the candidate
unanimously elect him king

they cheer from the back rows
of their very modern churches
risking all in voice and song
far less of their allegiance

in him expecting victory
from rome and incarceration
they wait not for the rocks to cry
but shout their present hope

until he speaks of peaceful kingdoms
far beyond the roman now
the problems come again to main street
of taxes, crime and strangers

they leave to buy their private homes
returning things to normal
talking they go home still talking
dreams, and donkeys, kings and things

and motley armies all in step
with failure and frustration
and see three wishes wasted trampled
like palms and coats they'd tossed away

and everything comes up snake eyes

Mark 12:1-11

monday tuesday wednesday

better by far than gold or silver finger cymbals
this coin of the realm clinking in our hands
sweet music for the real dance and business as usual

holy times are fine for children counting minutes
before birthdays but we make our dancing plans
with one eye on graphs marking growth and promise

good for business and politicians these holy days
allowing continual profits and housing starts
with briberies paid and guarantees made

sunday's exuberance is swept quietly under the counter
with the dried and brittle palms from the street
we do not begrudge parades as long as we come down to earth

HOLY WEEKS AND OTHER TIMES

Matthew 26:17-30

supper on thursday

we - with our ninety item salad bars
at all you dare eat low prices -
reading small print label lists
for unpronounceable ingredients
have difficulty at best
with simple bread and wine
offered with "for you" invitation

It asks the ultimate question
without concern for calories or cholesterol
is it i is it i is it i

eleven times we dip our bread
swallow it whole and lick our fingers clean
we close our satiated eyes
to those who wait outside with gaping mouths
so pleased with our private banquet
we avoid the question altogether
is it i is it i

then primary words are spoken
making up new covenants
giving simple gifts
of remission
forgiveness
of the question
is it i

John 19:16b-22, 25-30

friday

jesus speaks in seven lines
from the world's strangest stage
words complete with consequence
for seven days of every week

forgive he prays for those who do
but do not know the why the when or how
he knows they must all leave this hill
so asks possibility and godly grace

then thirsting with the drought of want
he tastes the vinegar of their wrongs
pressed on his dying lips they mock
and in his thirst he takes their own

he makes his promise to a thief
and other such anonymous ones
who hang on simple last chance hopes
with simple dreams of paradise

he cries for every midnight child
for parents with dead babes in arms
eloi he cries a foreign tongue *eloi*
translates forsakenness alone

he speaks to parents daughters sons
to open eyes to show them near
saying we have something to do with it all
beholding one another back in town

then with resignation tempered
with willingness he turns it over
to god so all in hope might
into such hands commend their spirits

one final shout *tetelestai*
a passive perfect finish once for all
their own incongruous shout of victory
the sure and total now amen

41

Psalm 22

echo

not so christ-crossed or forsaken

    (eloi eloi)

for others here and he

    (lema)

know and stand beside me

    (sabachthani)

John 20:24-31

saturday

pain banged against their eyes
with every move of the window blind
pulled tight against their fear
and the gathering storms outside
followers once they went nowhere now
except to cross the hideout room
to touch another weak with grief
shuddering with aftershocks from friday's quake
their shoulders shook rolling tears
down death grey cheeks
to fall with hopes and dreams
splattering on the wooden floor
while everyone looked for thomas

the women wept openly
more than the men who kept their secrets
huddled within passing questions
like players in macabre games of was
peter always one of ready voice
spoke pious quotes from ancient songs
in vain bravado he the rock
they stilled him with their silent stares
the reality of the day closed tighter
like stale and sweaty much used air
that filled their room of waiting
someone asked again for thomas

it was a day that sabbath day
without beginning without belonging
the friday time had done them in
they had only now their recollections
of what had been had been
with short and stuttered breaths of now
and wide-eyed fear of present tense
the made small guesses of what would be
each secretly wishing they could disappear
like thomas
wherever thomas was

HOLY WEEKS AND OTHER TIMES

John 21:15-19

sunday two

first it seemed like a ridiculous postscript
jotted not on the bottom of the page but on the back
not to be seen until the letter was
      flipped away almost covered by tomorrow's news

everything went sort of upside down
first the women's foolish report
then the peterjohn race straight to truth
      with one more head long blunder

it was as if we had lost our minds
emotional strain too much a drain
like we all needed vacations
      a couple of days out fishing

then the teacher came to meet us where we were
told us to leave the room and hit the streets
for resurrection meant nothing if it did not mean
      getting on with life and love and letting go

and the whole week seemed like a hand written letter
that needed reading and reading again

"The most satisfying thing in life is to have been able to give a large part of oneself to others."

Theillhard de Chardin

F O L L O W E R S

Luke 5:27-31; 19:1-10

a most recent matthew

comfortable
i sit behind my table
proper three feet wide
cheating them or myself
i am not sure

collecting
customs and taxes
from perfect strangers
who pass my table
on the acceptable other side

careful
scrupulous to a fault
i am safe
minimal contact allowed
i incline backwards and away

conscious
then i see him
slip behind my table
he moves it making
passage
to street cripples scabbed and dying

curiously
i wonder why
when they come in to touch me
it feels good to be included
i leave my table and meet the crowd

Isaiah 43:9

the minstrel sang
accepted songs
tuned to those who listened
for that is how a minstrel eats
but that's not how he dreams

the minstrel dreamed
his new note songs
humming humming humming
in his head the melody
to shock the monomoderntones
who knew three notes and never
sang in sequence

the minstrel sang
his private song
he knew its lilt and flow
would penetrate with loud cadenza
piercing dull conservachords
who played in precise form
and nonsense

the minstrel sang
accepted songs
until tired they requested
him to sing his practised song
no longer now in secret

FOLLOWERS

Philippians 2:8
Hebrews 4:14-16

wild roses

"not counting equality with god a thing
to be grasped, he humbled himself, and
became obedient to death..."

seeing only the bloom
the child reached in
pulled the rose from the stem
leaving tiny drops of blood
like last year's seeds
glistening from the thorns

he picked more
then brought a bouquet
risking the realities
for one simple fading gift
that would last a day or two
but longer in another's heart

Luke 21:1-4; 9:46-48

Bit Parts

There have been many,
almost anonymous,
certainly not famous,
somebodies
who played the triangle
in the school band.

Gentle ones, unloud
hardly even there
except to be a skip
in the march and overture
accenting the music,
a sparkle, a tiny star.

There have been many
tinkling somebodies
who give a glimpse of the God
who said, maybe of them,
"It is good, it is very good,
it is good they are here."

Reprinted by permission from Augsburg Fortress.

49

FOLLOWERS

John 8:1-11

euangelion (good news)

when church folk turn their earth
    tones to revelry
    and put flowers in their hair
the gospel squared and straight
gets all four corners knocked off
    thus and so
    quite naturally
    becomes more comfort
    able
    and much harder
    to measure
    in inches or in sins

Ephesians 2:19-22

(euloge) - Well-spoken

Share the cup of good words
    sweet as old old wine
    aged long in deep cellars.

Let the fragrance reach to all
    with wisps of prayer and peace
    spoken from an inner source.

Hear the words well spoken
    with incomparable warmth
    to the very centre

Of the heart. Pass the cup
    from old to young to old
    with brother/sister talk.

Share the wine of wooden thought
    shaped deliberately slow
    full of still rich truth.

Pass the holy cup, the one
    as old as hills, new as now
    ever today as the sun.

Touch the cup with open eyes
    on them, sunbrown, ancient,
    or pink as newborn babes.

Come and eat. Break the bread.
    Taste the words. Remember
    first and final feasts.

FOLLOWERS

Matthew 24:42-44

the little clown

the little clown with sad sad smile
warming his hands
on blown kisses
played main street

some did laugh
in spite of self
but more slipped by
on further sides
with turned heads

with fastened hearts
glanced back to see
if any noticed
then entered stores
with no intention

to buy some time
avoid the issue
ignore the clown
who waved balloons
in good word sign

his white death face
and blood red nose
not funny anymore
the truth he played
they never heard

the sad clown died
two children cried
a cripple too
and a grey old man
the city changed

but none knew why

"Joy is the serious business of heaven."

C.S. Lewis

CELEBRATIONS

Psalm 149:1-5
Luke 10:21

celebrations

they brought balloons to church
faces scowled round tsking tongues
the children giggled

three clowns tossed coloured balls
theologies were juggled around masks and hypocrites
the children laughed

they sang songs like happy birthdays
a few went tight lipped and wrinkled
the children clapped

they washed some feet and water spilled
heads shook loose whys from nervous eyes
the children splashed why nots

they told some funny stories
not all could understand
the children took them home

and wondered why celebrations are reserved
for julys or championships
and other victories

Isaiah 11:6-9

the juggler

flouter of laws
    of decency
    and decorum
this gregarious laugher
    at gravity
    tosses   clu
    kn   es   bs
        iv   and
    o   o   d   b   s
c   l   u   e   a   l
            r   l
against the sky
        then unnerves me
        by smiling through all
this impossible conglomeration

he draws my eyes
    to his irrational display
        and i don't notice anymore
            the mud i am standing in
                puddling around my feet

CELEBRATIONS

Matthew 20:1-16

potted plant

flowers on the altar
stand prim proper and pious
straight and severe
like silent worshippers
daring only slight fragrance
        on a passing wind of doctrine

i want each time i see them
to pick one or two
to risk
a full bouquet
just for you

but we don't do that
in our church
for we are wholly
            wholly
            wholly
proper amen

Psalm 126

joy notes

when they dropped the offering
during the duet
my personality split
right down the aisle
one part giggling with the children
the other frowning down
in righteous wrath
saying when order was restored
that is better
knowing all the while
it wasn't

CELEBRATIONS

Psalm 150

dances of the children

ubiquitous little children laugh
rings around my fears
i see their sunshine faces sparkle
through my salty tears
they hold my hands and circle
a ring the roses dance
husha husha we fall in hope
giving games a chance

Matthew 17:1-8

Transfigurations

One day, I spoke with Moses who stuttered.
        Yes, I did. I really did.
        My mother said, "Practice your piano."
Moses told how he was hid in a boat in the reeds,
        Then how a beautiful princess saved him.
        My father said, "Shovel the snow."
Moses did magic with his hand in his shirt,
        Then turned a stick to a snake on the ground.
        My teacher announced, "Homework is due tomorrow."
Moses led me through the gate past the backyard fence,
        Showed me a bush that sure looked on fire.
        A man with a microscope laughed.
Moses related tales of burning deserts, quail for supper.
        He laughed loud at Egyptian jokes.
        The billboard read, "Ten minutes to McDonalds."
Moses recounted a forty day mountaintop Godnear stay
        And of lifetimes lived in ten lines.
        My mind shouted, "Nonsense in your head."
It was just about then Elijah wheeled up in a chariot
        And invited me along for a ride.

INDICES

Scriptural Index

Genesis 1:31-2:3	6	Matthew 23:1-28	26
Genesis 8:18-22	3	Matthew 24:42-44	52
Exodus 16:1-12	22	Matthew 26:17-30	40
Numbers 14:1-9	23	Mark 10:13-16	17
Psalm 13	32-33	Mark 12:1-11	39
Psalm 22	42	Luke 1:23-28	12
Psalm 33:6-22	20	Luke 1:26-45	11
Psalm 37:7-11	21	Luke 5:27-31	46
Psalm 51	34-35	Luke 6:37-42	27
Psalm 126	57	Luke 9:46-48	49
Psalm 139:1-18	4	Luke 10:21	54
Psalm 149:1-5	54	Luke 19:1-10	46
Psalm 150	58	Luke 19:47-48	25
Isaiah 11:6-9	55	Luke 21:1-1	49
Isaiah 35	7	John 1:1-14	13
Isaiah 42:18-22;43:1-13	15	John1:14	18
Isaiah 43:9	47	John 8:1-11	50
Isaiah 61:1-9	16	John 19:16b-22, 25-30	41
Jeremiah 26	25	John 20:24-31	43
Jeremiah 33:6-11	2	John 21:15-19	44
Jeremiah 35:15-17	14	Romans 14:1-13	30
Ezekiel 13:10-16	24	1 Corinthians 11:27-29	28
Amos 6:1-6	29	Galatians 5:1	8
Matthew 1:14	14	Ephesians 2:19-22	51
Matthew 1:18-25	11	Ephesians 4:1-16	5
Matthew 11:28-30	17	Philippians 2:8	48
Matthew 17:1-8	59	Colossians 3:12-17	9
Matthew 20:1-16	56	Hebrews 4:14-16	48
Matthew 21:1-11	38	1 Peter 1:3-9	36-37
Matthew 22:39	29	Revelation 21:1-5a	6

Liturgical Index

Advent	11,12,15,16	Palm Sunday	38
Christmas	6,12,13,14,	Maundy Thursday	40
	15,16,17,18	Good Friday	41,42
Lent	20,22,23,32-33,	Easter Vigil	43
	34-35,36-37,38,39,40	Easter	44
Ash Wednesday	32-33,34-35	Pentecost	9
Holy Week	39,43	Trinity	2

Agape	52	Imagination	5,8
Annunciation	11	Incarnation	13,15,16,18,40
Awareness	29	Inclusion	46,58
Broken tradition	47,56,57	Individuals, celebration of	49
Celebration	8,36-37,39,44,	Inspiration	59
	50, 54,55,57,58	Intolerance	32-33
Challenges	47,55	Joy	54
Change	59	Justice	21,29
Children	58	Laughter	50
Comfort	17,42	Longings	7
Commission	44	Losing life	48
Commitment	25,52	Love	48
Community	40,51	New life	18
Compassion	46	Prejudice	5,7,28,30,46,50
Confession	20,21,26,29,	Presence of God	18
	32-33 ,34-35,40	Reconciliation	3
Conformity	5,8	Recreation	4
Creation	2,6,18	Rededication	3
Creativity	4,5,7,8,9,47	Redemption	4,6,7,15,16,24
Crucifixion	41,42	Rejuvenation	4
Death	36-37	Repentence	20,22,24,26,
Dedication	22,55		32-33,34-35,42
Denial	21	Reservation	56
Discipleship	23,46,47	Resurrection	36-37,44
Doubt	23,43	Revelation	11,59
Environmental concerns	2,3	Risk	25,47,48,52
Eternal life	44	Sacrifice	48
Eucharist	9,28,40,51	Self-centeredness	29
Examination	28	Self-donation	52
Expectations	38	Self-examination	27
False security	24,27,30,39	Self-righteousness	26
Fear	43	Self-worth	49
Forgiveness	34-35,41	Seven last words of Christ	41
Freedom	5,8,24	Shared faith	56
Gifts	49,56	Sharing	51
God's activity	2	Sin, effects of	2,3,6,7,13,16,21
God's love	6	Society	21
Grief	43,52	Surprise	12,13,17,44
Guilt	21,34-35	Transfiguration	59
Holy Spirit	4,9,24	Truth	25,27,36-37
Hope	7,14,15,17,	Ungratefulness	22
	18,36- 37,58	Violence	2
Hypocrisy	14,26	Worship	50,54,56,57

A B O U T   T H E   P O E T

David Kaiser, a native of Iowa, came to Canada in 1961. He has had an interest in writing since childhood. He became interested in poetry when his grade seven English teacher assigned poems to be memorized. Finding it easier to write than memorize, David began practicing the art, and has continued for the past twenty years. Influenced by e.e. cummings, David likes the freedom poetry brings both the writer and the reader. David has had several poems published in various magazines and has given public readings to High School and University English classes.

Besides poetry, David also writes short stories, plays, drama/dialogues and Bible study courses. His Grade 9 - Spring quarter of the **Rejoice** Sunday School course was published by Augsburg-Fortress. The video **"All About Community"**, written by Kaiser and produced by the Office of Resource Development of the ELCIC was completed in 1992. It features David's puppets which are one of his many other interests.

David presently holds the position of Chaplain at Luther College, University of Regina. David and his wife Marlys have four children and four grandchildren, who often are subjected to the first drafts.